2

3

M E R C Y

By

John C Burt.

6

Photographs Courtesy of :
   thomas - kinto.
   seyedeh - hamideh.
   priscilla - du - preez.
   mohamed - nohassi.
   mars - caveman.
   gift - habeshaw.

Free Downloads on :
   unsplash.com

(C) Copyright to John C Burt 2020. Words and text.

DO
estly
love
ercy
walk
mbly
Micah 6:8

1.

FOREWORD :

The title of this very book is ' Mercy ' and it would seem

to me in these dark days ... we all need the very Mercy of the Lord Jesus Christ more and more .. Like never before !

Mercy is seen by some as a form of weakness and they have problems , some very real problems in the asking of God to show Mercy? I would be of the belief that as we cry out to the Lord Jesus Christ, He will in reality show Mercy !

May be you are a person who finds it hard to believe a god, the One True God, the Lord Jesus Christ, the very Son of God can in reality show Mercy? I would encourage you more and more to cry out to the Lord Jesus Christ for Mercy .. and much more of it!

This book on Mercy, will focus primarily on Micah 6 : 6 - 12. Mercy is something which the Lord Jesus Christ, and The Father and the Holy Spirit require us to show to others. This is in terms of right Worship of the Godhead, the Father, the Son and the Holy Spirit !

While the book will be primarily concerned with Micah 6 : 6 - 12 and the requirement of showing Mercy.

I want to use this as a springboard to think and discuss more and more about the quality of Mercy. Also, to actively think about our very need to cry out for the Lord Jesus Christ to show Mercy to us all , in the world - at -

large in these dark days of Covid - 19? But also, in relation to the what may come in the world - at - large , our world ?

So strap yourself in, and be prepared to engage your brain ... and think through the very real need for Mercy to be shown and also for Mercy to be received from the Lord Jesus Christ !

DO
stly
love
ercy
walk
mbly
Micah 6:8

2.

In this chapter and the ones that follow the very texts that this book will consider will be cited. Four different versions of the texts will be cited, that is, the ESV, the NIV, the Voice and the GNT.

{ ESV }

MICAH 6 : 6 - 12.

WHAT DOES THE LORD REQUIRE ?

" (6) " With what shall I come before the LORD,

and bow myself before God on high?
    Shall I come before him with burnt offerings, with calves a year old?
    (7) Will the LORD be pleased with....

thousands of rams, with ten thousands of rivers of oil? Shall I give my firstborn for my transgression, the fruit of my body for the sin of my soul?"

44

(8) He has told you, O man, what is good; and what does the LORD require of you
    but to do justice, and to love kindness, and to walk humbly with your

God?

(9) The voice of the LORD cries to the city - and it is sound wisdom to fear your name: " Hear of the rod and of him who appointed it!

(10) Can I forget any longer the treasures of wickedness in the house of the wicked, and the scant measure that is accursed?

(11) Shall I acquit the man with wicked scales

and with a bag of deceitful weights? (12) Your rich men are full of violence; your inhabitants speak lies, and their tongue is deceitful in their mouth." "

Micah 7 : 16 - 19.

" (16) The nations shall see and be ashamed of all their might; they shall lay their hands on their mouths; they ears shall be deaf;

(17) they shall lick the dust like a serpent, like the crawling things of the earth; they shall come trembling out of their strongholds; they

shall turn in dread to the LORD our God, and they shall be in fear of you.

(18) Who is a God like you, pardoning iniquity and passing over transgression for the remnant of ...

his inheritance? He does not retain his anger forever, because he delights in steadfast love.

(19) He will again have compassion on us; he will tread our iniquities underfoot.

You will cast all our sins into the depths of the sea."

Psalm 123.

" (1) To you I lift up my eyes, O you who are enthroned in the heavens!

(2) Behold, as the eyes of servants look to the hand of their master, as the eyes of a maidservant to the hand of her mistress, so our eyes look to the

LORD our God, till he has mercy upon us.

(3) Have mercy upon us, O LORD have mercy upon us, for we have had more than enough of contempt.

(4) Our soul has had more than enough of the scorn of those who are at ease, of the contempt of the proud."

DO
stly
love
ercy
walk
nbly
Micah 6:8

3.

{ NIV }

Micah 6 : 6 - 12.

" (6) With what shall I come before the LORD and bow down before the exalted God? Shall I come before him with burnt offerings, with calves a year old?

(7) Will the LORD be pleased with thousands of rams, with then thousand rivers of olive oil? Shall I offer my firstborn for my transgression, the fruit of my body for the sin of my

soul?

(8) He has shown you, O mortal, what is good. And what does the LORD require of you? To act justly and to love mercy and to walk humbly with your God.

(9) Listen! The LORD is calling to the city - and to fear your name is wisdom -
" Heed the rod and the One who appointed it.
(10) Am I still to forget your ill - gotten .....

treasures , you wicked house, and the short ephah, which is accursed?

(11) Shall I acquit someone with dishonest scales, with a bag of false weights?

(12) Your rich people are violent; your inhabitants are liars and their tongues speak deceitfully. " "

Micah 7 : 16 - 19.

"(16)Nations will see and be ashamed, deprived of all their power. They will put their hands over their mouths and their ears will become deaf.

(17) They

will lick dust like a snake, like creatures that crawl on the ground. They will come trembling out of their dens; they will turn in fear to the LORD our God and will be afraid of you. (18) Who is a God like you, who pardons sin and forgives the transgression of the remnant of his inheritance? You do not stay angry forever but delight to show mercy.

(19) You will again have compassion on us; you will tread our sins underfoot and hurl all our iniquities into the

depths of the sea."

Psalm 123.

A song of ascents.
" (1) I lift up my eyes to you, to you who sit enthrones in

heaven.

(2) As the eyes of slaves look to the hand of their master, as the eyes of a female slave look to the hand of her mistress, so our eyes look to the LORD our God, till

he shows us his mercy.

(3) Have mercy on us, LORD, have mercy on us, for we have endured no end of contempt.

(4) We have endured no end of

ridicule from the arrogant, of contempt from the proud."

DO
stly
love
rcy
walk
bly
cah 6.8

4.

{ The Voice }

Micah 6 : 6 - 12.

ISRAEL :

" (6) What should I bring into the presence of the Eternal One to pay homage to the God Most High? Should I come into His presence with burnt offerings, with year - old calves to sacrifice?

    (7) Would the Eternal be pleased by thousands of sacrificial rams, by ten thousand

swollen rivers of sweet olive oil? Should I offer my oldest son for my wrongdoing, the child of my body to cover the sins of my life?

(8) No. He has told you, mortals, what is

good in His sight. What else does the Eternal ask of you

    But to live justly and to love kindness and to walk with your True God in all humility?

(9) The voice of the Eternal cries out to the city of Jerusalem. and the wise fear Your name.

ETERNAL ONE :
  Listen, all of you gathered there,
    (tribe and people)

(10) Can I overlook the treasures of wickedness Stored away in the house of wicked, the dishonest scales and measures that I hate ?

(11) Can I overlook the one who uses crooked scales and bags of dishonest weights to cheat the innocent?

(12) Her rich are filled with violence, her citizens speak lies,

and the words of their mouths can never be trusted."

Micah 7 : 16 - 19.

" (16) The nations will see and be ashamed, despite all their might. With their hands over their mouths and ears they will hear nothing.

    (17) They will lick dust like the snakes of the earth crawling across the dirt. They will creep out of their holes,

shivering in terror because of You.

They turn to the Eternal, our True God, filled with dread, and they stand in awe of You.

(18) Is there any other

God like You, who forgives evil
    and passes over the transgressions done by Yours who remain?
    He does not hold onto His anger forever because He delights in showing love and kindness.

(19) He will take pity on us again, will tread our wrongdoing underfoot. He will cast all our sins down to the bottom of the sea."

Psalm 123.

" (1) I raise my eyes to fix my gaze on You, for Your throne resides in the heavens.

(2) Just as the eyes of servants closely watch the hand of

their masters,
Just as a
maid carefully
observes the
slightest gesture
of her mistress,
In the same
way we look to
You, Eternal One,
waiting for our

God to pour out His mercy upon us.

    (3) O Eternal One, show us Your mercy. We beg You.

    We are not strangers to contempt and pain.

(4) We have suffered more than our share of ridicule and contempt from self - appointed critics who live easy lives and pompously display their own importance."

Do
estly
love
ercy
walk
mbly
Micah 6:8

5.

{ GNT }

Micah 6 : 6 - 12.

What the LORD Requires:
    " (6) What shall I bring to the LORD, the God of heaven, when I come to worship him? Shall I bring the best calves to burn as offerings to him?

(7) Will the LORD be pleased if I bring him thousands of sheep or endless streams of olive oil? Shall I offer him my first - born

child to pay for my sins?

(8)No, the LORD has told us what is good. What he requires of us is this: to do what is just, to show constant love, and to live in humble fellowship with ...

our God.

(9) It is wise to fear the LORD. He calls to the city, " Listen, you people who assemble in the city!

(10) In the houses of ...

evil people are treasures which they got dishonestly. They use false measures, a thing I hate.

(11) How can I forgive those who use false scales and weights?

(12) Your rich people exploit the poor, and all of you are liars."

Micah 7 : 16 - 19.

" (16) The nations will see this and be frustrated in spite of all their strength. In dismay they will close their mouths and cover their ears.
(17) They

will crawl in the dust like snakes; they will come from their fortresses, trembling and afraid. They will turn in fear to the LORD our God.

118

(18) There is no other god like you, O LORD; you forgive the sins of your people who have survived. You do not stay angry forever, but you take pleasure in showing us your

constant love. (19) You will be merciful to us once again. You will trample our sins underfoot and send them to the bottom of the sea ! "

Psalm 123.

" (1) LORD, I look up to you, up to heaven, where you rule.

(2) As a servant depends on his master, as a maid depends

on her mistress, so we will keep looking to you, O LORD our God, until you have mercy on us.

(3) Be merciful to us, LORD, be merciful; we have been treated with

so much contempt.

    (4) We have been mocked too long by the rich and scorned by proud oppressors."

DO
estly
love
ercy
walk
mbly
Micah 6:8

6.

To start with we will give some consideration to Micah 6 : 6 - 12?

The question that is hypothetically asked right from the outset of these verses , sets the tone for what follows ? It

is as follows :
' What shall I bring to the LORD, the God of heaven, when I come to worship him?' { GNT } In the end, the answer to this question is caught up with the showing and the ..

very receiving of MERCY ! What in the end, can I or we bring to the Lord God Almighty ... who is so high and mighty, He is the LORD GOD ALMIGHTY ..far above us as His ..

creations.

    In these days of Covid - 19 it is in reality, the right question to be asking and in fact it is the right question to be asking at any time. There is such a thing as ..

' right and true ' worship of the Lord God Almighty? At times, we are in danger , even in our days and in our generations of coming before the Lord God Almighty to seek to worship Him with the wrong attitude and not in a way that is in anyway worshipful! I say this, because I do not want you to think that it is not a question that we have to deal with?

In the days of Micah, they were trusting in the sacrificial system ... the system of sacrifices and offerings that made it possible for them to come before and even approach the Lord God Almighty in worship ... Yet, in saying even this , one has to note and remember that the Lord God Almighty looks upon the heart ?

Remember that in their world view it was the very heart of a person that was at the very center of the person and individual ... In our days, and in our generations the Lord God Almighty still looks at the heart of a person as they come before Him in worship, or even as they seek to do this ?

Verse 7 details further things that we can seek to give the Lord God Almighty as we come before in Worship ... They are largely external things...

and removed from the heart and it's attitude before the Lord God Almighty. Then as now, we can seek to make so - called sacrifices to the Lord God Almighty and yet not come before the Lord God Almighty with the right attitude of heart!

Let us now consider verse 8; {NIV} ' He has shown you, O ...

mortal, what is good. And what does the LORD require of you? To act justly and to love mercy and to walk humbly with your God.' This verse from the outset gets the relations right; we are the creatures , the mortals and the Lord God Almighty is the Creator. In the end, we are not the Lord God Almighty and are not gods ?

The two things that the verse deals with as being needed as one comes before the Lord God Almighty in worship have to do with CHARACTER! They are actions, things we do, they are verbs, doing words ... This is what the Lord God Almighty requires of those who come before Him in an attitude of WORSHIP ! All of which relates primarily to the heart and it's attitudes ... As they say , 'actions speak louder than your words?'

'To act justly and to love mercy' are connected and in

some ways , flow out of each other. Micah , like many of the Prophets , was calling the people of the Lord God Almighty back to deeds that were righteous and in accordance with both the commands of the Lord God Almighty and His revealed will, as was made known to them through the Scriptures and the Prophets themselves.

The bottom line that comes out of all of this, is that, if one wants to be shown MERCY by the Lord God Almighty, then one needs to be showing and even walking in MERCY towards others? The question to be asked, is how merciful am I ? We serve, worship and follow the Lord Jesus Christ and we need to be merciful and walk in the very dynamic of mercy being shown to others in our lives. The Lord Jesus Christ said as much in the Gospels of …

the New Testament ... Being MERCIFUL and showing the attribute of MERCY is a requirement that the Lord Jesus Christ of those who would follow after HIM !

I would believe that the crescendo of the final part of verse 8 ; ' and to walk humbly with your God' ; comes out of and is intimately ....

connected with
the showing of
MERCY ...

MERCY +
HUMILITY =
RIGHT WORSHIP
OF THE LORD
GOD ALMIGHTY !

Sadly, at times

we have largely forgotten the very real need for HUMILITY BEFORE THE LORD GOD ALMIGHTY AND OUR FELLOW MAN ? Humility and mercy go together, they in fact feed off each other ...All of which comes back to the hypothetical question of verse 6 ....' With what shall I come before the LORD?' We need to have a heart that is both merciful and full of humility as we seek to come before the LORD GOD ALMIGHTY, in an attitude of worship, reverence and awe .... That is, in the end, RIGHT WORSHIP OF THE LORD GOD ALMIGHTY !

The rest of the verses cited from Micah 6 : 6 - 12 have to do with the opposite of doing things justly and showing mercy and even humbly with the Lord God Almighty. There is a very contrast between verse 8 and it call to act and behave justly , to show mercy and to walk humbly with the Lord God Almighty in the very real behaviors the very people of the Lord

God Almighty were in fact doing and being known to be doing .. Remember that Micah, is a still a Prophet , one who is calling the people of the Lord God Almighty back to ' right ' behavior.

DO
...stly
love
...rcy
...valk
...bly
...ah 6:8

7.

Let us now give consideration to Micah 7 : 16 - 19 and what it has to say to us about MERCY ?

One again, has to remember that Micah is Prophet and is speaking Prophecy ... it is a clear verdict against the very nations .. His language is stronger than we have expected .. and yet it comes from the very Heart of the Lord God Almighty .. When it happens , is debatable and whether or not it has successive fulfillment , is another question we need to think about? All of this indictment ends with the nations turning to the Lord God Almighty ' in fear'. Which in

the end, leads into the very cry for MERCY from the Lord God Almighty? As can be seen in the words of verse 18; ' Who is a God like you ...
 You do not stay angry forever but

delight to show mercy.' In the end, it is all caught up with very CHARACTER of the LORD GOD ALMIGHTY .. He DELIGHTS to SHOW MERCY ... For a moment , think about that,

HE DELIGHTS TO SHOW MERCY ... Think about the words, DELIGHTS TO SHOW MERCY ! It is not just that He likes or enjoys showing MERCY but rather that He ..

DELIGHTS TO SHOW MERCY ..
  Delights to show MERCY to both His people and the nations of the earth .. MERCY is a quality that does in reality define His very ......
190

CHARACTER ..
DELIGHTS to
SHOW MERCY !
 All the more
reason for us as
follower's of the
Lord Jesus Christ
to show and walk
in real MERCY
towards ourselves
and others !

Verse 19, fills out for us what this MERCY, shown to the people of the Lord God Almighty, the Father, the Son and the Holy Spirit looks like and is defined by? In the end, we need to remember that we are dealing with a Lord God Almighty who is in reality a God who is HOLY ! He cannot , because of His own HOLINESS turn a blind eye to all our sin and wrongdoing and that of the Nations ... It rather that He has compassion on us and this is truer for the people of the Lord God Almighty POST - CROSS ... The Death of the Son of God, the LORD JESUS CHRIST upon the very CROSS of CALVARY paid ...

for all our sins and our wrongdoing before the gaze of the Father, the Lord God Almighty. All of which, is in the end caught up with the compassionate provision of the

Father ... to make a way back to Him. ... A way and means of atoning for our sins and our wrongdoing ... making things right before the Father, the very Father of the Lord

Jesus Christ.

    All of which, speaks into the current crisis surrounding Covid - 19 and it's impact upon the world - at - large. He is still the Father who has ...

and had MERCY and COMPASSION upon the world - at - large , through the provision and the very sending of His own Son, the Lord Jesus Christ into the world - at - large and ultimately ..

leading to the very Cross of Calvary ...He died upon that very Cross of Calvary in My, Our, Everybody's place ... He by this made a way back to the Father, His very own Father ...

   Therefore ; in the very Cross of Calvary, we see the MERCY and COMPASSION of the Father, the Son of God, the Lord Jesus Christ and the Holy Spirit displayed in large letters!

DO
stly
love
ercy
walk
nbly
icah 6:8

8.

Finally, we will give .... consideration to Psalm 123 : 1 - 4 and what it has to say about MERCY ?

214

DO
stly
love
ercy
walk
nbly
icah 6:8

A song of ascents : Psalm 123 {NIV}

"(1) I lift up my eyes to you, to you who sit enthroned in heaven. (2) As the ..

eyes of slaves look to the hand of their master; as the eyes of a female slave look to the hand of her mistress, so our eyes look to the LORD our

God, till he shows us his mercy.

(3) Have mercy on us, LORD, have mercy on us, for we have endured no end of contempt.

(4) We have endured no end of ridicule from the arrogant, of contempt from the proud."

In terms of our ongoing discussion of MERCY in this book, we come to this particular verses. It's opening

words are profound in themselves ;
 ' (1) I lift up my eyes to you, to you who sit enthroned in heaven.' The source of any and all MERCY we may want comes from HEAVEN and THE

LORD GOD ALMIGHTY ! From what we have already seen in this very book, the Lord God Almighty, the Father, the Son and the Holy Spirit; have already shown us

all amazing
MERCY and
COMPASSION in
and through the
Coming and the
Death and the
ultimate
RESURRECTION
from the Dead of
the Lord Jesus
Christ. I have a

desire and even a need to make that plain from the very outset as we discuss Psalm 123 : 1 - 4?

All of which, is summed up in verse 2 b : ' ... so

our eyes look to the LORD our God, till he shows us his mercy.' This is , in some ways a continuation of the very thoughts broached in verse 1 about the Lord God Almighty!

The words that proceed these words, make us akin to slaves who are looking towards their Master, and their Mistress for both direction and in this case MERCY and COMPASSION.

You may or may not think the word pictures of slaves is apt , I don't know where you are at in your following of the Lord Jesus Christ? But in the end, this image holds with the rest of the Word of God, and in particular the New Testament and it's writings and very contents and themes? As a case in point, think about how the Lord Jesus Christ could refer to us ..

230

as SERVANTS just doing the bidding of their MASTER, The Father, the very Son of God, the Lord Jesus Christ and the Holy Spirit.

 Verse 3 : ' Have mercy on us,

LORD, have mercy on us, for we have endured no end of contempt.' To a degree, one could see this as referring to the way and ways that follower's of the Lord Jesus

Christ are viewed today ... Even, in the midst of this current crisis .. Covid - 19 ... Some people have utter contempt both for the Name of the Lord Jesus Christ and those who Follow Him!

However, we are the very Ones who can cry out for the Lord God Almighty to show MERCY and COMPASSION amidst this very real crisis of Covid - 19?   A few examples from the past weeks will make this whole thing of the very cries of the People of the Lord Jesus Christ being answered in real ways and in real terms are as ...

follows :

A man who was 97 years old , fully recovered the other day from Covid - 19 and was released from Hospital in Italy ....

There was also the case of two sisters in Spain, who both had contracted Covid - 19 and who recovered and were reunited as sisters in the hospital .....

I would also see the large numbers of people who recovered from the Covid - 19 virus ... it is in the 100,000 thousands ... Something which the nightly news on the television does not major on and even highlight as something which is in reality in itself NEWSWORTHY !

In the end, the very words of verse 3 are the ones I want to conclude this very chapter on :
' (1) Have mercy on us, LORD, have mercy on us, '

I would in the end, that this is the very cry of the Body of Christ Worldwide for the World - at - Large that the Father loves so much that He sent the Son to it!

DO
estly
love
ercy
walk
mbly
Micah 6:8

9.

EPILOGUE:

DO
stly
love
rcy
walk
nbly
icah 6.8

I wonder how in the end sum up a book on MERCY?

In the end, all I want to do is to quote some of

the verses we have thought about :
Micah 6 : 8
{ NIV}
 " (8) He has shown you, O mortal, what is

good. And what does the LORD require of you? To act justly and to love mercy and to walk humbly with your God."

Psalm 123 : 3
{ NIV }
" (3) Have mercy on us, LORD, have mercy on us, ..."

Both these verses seem to be a very real way of summing up this book called " MERCY "? In these times with Covid - 19 and beyond we as the Body of Christ need to be crying out for the MERCY of the Lord God Almighty!

DO
stly
love
ercy
walk
nbly
Micah 6:8

The Author:

JOHN C BURT.

274

JOHN HAS BEEN A FOLLOWER OF THE LORD JESUS CHRIST FOR FORTY-THREE YEARS!

JOHN LOVES PIZZA, COFFEE AND CHICKEN AND JELLYFISH, BEST SERVED COLD OR CHILLED !

JOHN LOVES AND I MEAN LOVES ANY FORM OR TYPE OF SPORT , USUALLY INVOLVING ..

278

TEAMS .... ATHLETICS IS A PARTICULAR FONDNESS OF JOHN'S ... RUNNING RACES ....

AMEN and AMEN...

SHALOM:

DEAR LORD JESUS CHRIST;

WE CRY OUT TO YOU TO SHOW MERCY UPON US IN THE WORLD ..

YOU WERE SENT TO DIE FOR. MAY WE ACT JUSTLY AND LOVE TO SHOW MERCY, JUST AS YOU SHOW MERCY!

HELP US TO GET OUR ACTIONS AND OUR HEARTS RIGHT BEFORE YOU THE FATHER

AND THE HOLY SPIRIT. THANKS THAT YOU ARE A LORD GOD ALMIGHTY WHO IS MERCIFUL! AMEN !!!

DO
stly
love
ercy
walk
nbly
icah 6.8

298

299

300

301

CPSIA information can be obtained
at www.ICGtesting.com
Printed in the USA
LVHW012310210420
654156LV00007B/478